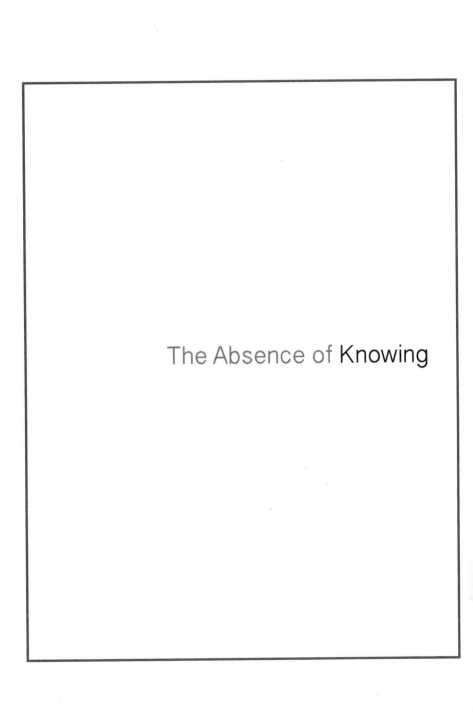

The Absence of Knowing

The Absence of Knowing

Matthew Henriksen

Black Ocean
Boston · Detroit · Chicago

Black Ocean
P.O. Box 52030
Boston, MA 02205
blackocean.org

Cover Art and Design by Janaka Stucky | janakastucky.com
Book Design by Nikkita Cohoon | nikkita.co

ISBN 978-1-939568-13-7

Library of Congress Cataloging-in-Publication Data

Names: Henriksen, Matthew.
Title: The absence of knowing / Matthew Henriksen.
Description: Boston : Black Ocean, 2015.
Identifiers: LCCN 2015041445 | ISBN 9781939568137 (alk. paper)
Classification: LCC PS3608.E56455 A6 2015 | DDC 811/.6-dc23
LC record available at http://lccn.loc.gov/2015041445

FIRST EDITION

for Kaveh Bassiri

The fact that we find Lascaux beautiful means that Babylon has at last begun to fall.

—Hakim Bey

Contents

I

II

III

IV

V

I

Baby

I

Bring the fatted worm to the altar
I will pin down the skin

The body open
What you imagined

An orphan cannot say her father is no man
A worm cannot say

No No Don't do this
But the fatted baby will say

When she is older I don't remember
What my father cut from me

II

At the back of each eye
I see a future without automobiles

Save two chestnut Ford Mavericks
In an abandoned salvage yard

Well after my child has died I will see the sun
As it will be on the backs of those cars

In the beginning of this new
And ancient and only reality

III

I can hardly bring myself to flip the blinker
I can hardly turn the wheel right

If I break down
Like the sun weeps

My child will hear the arietta
In Beethoven's last sonata

And an image will strike my child's eye
Optimistic beyond repair

The day will squeeze
All that is holy from the body

And set it down like a fish on a rock
Under the sun's violence

Sweetness and Milk

I mostly raised myself
I've been told

My mother taught me sliced bananas
In a bowl with sugar and milk
So I practiced taking the bowl from the cabinet
I practiced quiet in the kitchen

Summer evenings I crossed the lawn
Into the street barefoot and practiced
Every nerve detecting every particle

I practiced projecting against the sky
The air felt cooler and the clouds
Seemed less against me

I knew people would ruin me for a new car

Before I learned sex, whiskey, and debt
I knew the two hungers

One licks the sugar
The other holds the bowl

Stereo Gone

Today my daughter shouted to where
A mourning dove nested on her window ledge

When it flew away we saw two eggs

I wonder what Lao Tzu would say

How little I think

Light will not flame
When I hold a match to it
But might have once
Before my brother the inmate shriveled inward
Though still with all his teeth

Once the happy genius
Coming down in the basement at five AM

His laughing
Like God laughing birds

Like my daughter laughed
As the bird lifted
Away like a balloon
Her arms reaching after
Its smallness

Her voice
Incremental in the distances

Requiem For Now

Try
I tell myself

Not to impose a narrative
When I cannot see where my wife looks in a mirror

Our first plan belonged to us
Our daughter protests for eggs
Her feet tiny heart bird claws

Our second plan belonged to marriage
Where blood circles the moon
We liked to live in the open parts of plants

I don't need to tell a story

My daughter laughs out a window's mouth
Talks like trying to count the air
Her repetition wringing worry out

Therapy Poem

My wife on the couch last night called me out on Breton

We don't talk about these things
It's milk and our daughter's attitude
Or I stare at the wall and think
Horse particles

Or I start to think
Horseshit
Or my wife says it
Only my wife never says
Horseshit

She looks at me with her eyes
And I think I am saying horseshit

The night she said let's watch *Persona*
We got through the opening sequence
Then our daughter woke up

We agree every morning on coffee
We eat the same meals
Share a toilet

Variations of happy sounded out in time
Animals animals and sleep

We do this thing when one of us plays Nina Simone
We both listen and sooner or later we start talking about her

I beg my wife to read Clarice Lispector
I do not know how to tell her about Celan

Silence of a gun versus silence of an afternoon
Or
Our silence asleep
A perfect film we never see
The tension of the split dream
Merged in one version of absence

I Throw Rocks

If you need a friend whose wings have lost their speed, find me behind the planetarium. We can throw rocks until the Zippo explodes. Once I watched two willows divorce and flare up into angels singing Hell Hymns to gasoline as they ascended into separate space stations in the dark. Where you dock matters to old friends. Your family might not recognize you in the space suit, but your new neighbors will appreciate your honesty, or your naivety, whatever charms them longest and makes you bearable in a shared atmosphere. As with all meetings, our first rule will not end. After that, attempts at authority allow us only to collapse upon each other. Sex often interrupts ideas. We close our eyes and imagine fire in aluminum containers, which generate variations of sounds we sought as a forgotten memory, a hazy but formidable blank, a piece missing from a light fixture in the room where we slept, and, though we did not grow up together, the color from a lost photograph we want to take over again.

We will repeat many of the same words. We cheat language. Our tongues discuss tactile noise. Kissing is cute, yes, while listening to our sweaters. Our child sleeps in the other room and even the silence hears her alien dreams. She, alligator or snowflake, chases the neighborhood dogs. All her dreams have animals, which allows us to live together undisturbed through the choking labyrinths of adulthood, toward the end of the maze with cobwebbed and shredded fabric walls. What has become of the divorce we fleeted? Rocks and dust everywhere. Our parents left us here, and now the empty room is ours. We sleep. We drink water. We fight. We go on missions for soap and dentistry. How obscenely we wean ourselves from circumstance and birth anew. You find mistletoe up in the elms, and I find hollyhocks inside a river inside a book. You laugh at gumball seeds on the sidewalk, and our daughter shrieks at each crescent moon.

We emerge from our apartment and rattle down the highway in our broken car. You point out hawks, hundreds of hawks. Our daughter sings "Salt Peanuts!" and solos Charlie Parker. No one knows what notes hide in another's head or where in our brains' photomorphic pastures our thoughts hide and play or where they divide or if there is division at all. An ear infection turns into the realization that I do not need a style, only to move and watch the formations of time, of sound, and of color and shape. The light now, in our dark living room, where I type with one exhausted eye on my phone, does not reach through the open door to you and our daughter asleep in the next room. I am no longer sick with fire or bad ideas. I put on my glasses and write with two eyes and two thumbs. As the heating fan shuts off I can hear the throb again in my bad ear. Still sick with infection, I move through time by writing down what faces me.

Sober Lullaby

Oak tree in time this story makes no recognition
A photo does not distance music caught in a wind
That entered the room where the child slept

Before she understood the word for tree she had one in mind
I dreamed a cold barroom
Every photo a song the mind dances inside

Break off that now the child breathes but does not wake
What happens to our girl does not happen to a tree
Music does not happen unless listening turns to breath
Little rooms when quiet recall failure

In this buzzing left over from another room
In this coffin I kiss my daughter in her sleep

II

People Say This Is Not Music

Quarter to eight sun cold ball of wax
Bedroom shape-shifting again
Nothing trembles under the low spot of each atom

I sit on a small chair and imagine
Clarinet divorced from time
My wife's boots no longer the boots in "The Dead"
But sprawled across the carpet titanic boats
Resting interminably in a desert

While cold in this room with indecently swinging piano
People say this is not music

Tell me type a head back into time
So people who watch television can follow
Room not too big, small room
Sheet music, stereo music, ear music, bird screams

I get on my knees I hear
Cracked bird claws on the windowsill sing

In the small teased out words
From a toothpaste tube language resembles prayer
For the people who say this is not prayer
Sucking up victuals from a grave in the hypothalamus
Their thirst will not deliver them from internet radio
Their stars will not grieve their transmogrifications
Ears folding a hermit crab's shell around the face
In middling lives they walk into trees
And hear the dull thud of stomach kissing mouth
To swallow something soft and tasteless

Opposite falling asleep I have taken
Seeds from my socks and fallen asleep
Insistent on the backward word shape
Screams back out bird wings
Above a stalled car on the street below

Strange Flowers

I

I found these Things to sum beyond us

A girl on a bicycle
The edges of her dress
Not touching a Thing
Apart from her body and a part of light

As a dream interns but does not part the day
Little does not belong
Even her eyes darkened in removal
From our longing to see ourselves seen

Too see a girl on a bicycle
Returns the mind
To the impulse of its hive

Glory of numbers
Internally beyond identity

II

In the street's inner shell
Under oak
Under sycamore
We watch memory
Perpetuate infinitely
No velocity

No direction
No naming locutions
The names of fathers devolve into faces
The names of mothers devolve into faces
As the faces of strangers devolve
And children appear

Each morning concomitant with or without birdsong
Though hardly ever without birdsong

Even in tired commutes
My mind vibrates abstractly
Daylight splints the spine
Mute and obligatorily answers the grass
Mirror to the eyes' begetting

Around these Things silence revolves
Strange flowers I do not know
The girl verging with the vanishing point
Horizons sinking slowly on their centers

My W/hole Aesthetic

"Walt Whitman."

Rust on the balcony, leaves. The trees are made of scratch-scratch. Terror of the leaf raking over concrete. I am trying to destroy my way out of Blake. Walt says, "I," and it is so. I am tired of talking about I, defending I. Accept it all.

Send something south and it blooms.

We wrote in a rapture of distress. Self-destruction. Not I-destruction. Went south and found an unmarked grave, now marked, two birth dates, a wedding day, awaiting the second day of death. I am god. Good, too. Good to you. For good. For ground. In a rapture of distress we unwrote ourselves and wrote a Self, receptacle of God, larks, lungs, longitudes, dung, and dogs. The barking of the howl, the day of the night, the sleep of the sun. Tomorrow we woke alone and I sat on the floor all morning, staring at a finch an hour. It came as far as the television table, perching for many minutes in silence—silences be damned, this was silence—aware of me completely and unafraid, flying away never fearing. Self-destruction leads to a lack of emitting fear, all fears admitted and culpably calculated in the lungs, where in choked breath a waking blackness comes, the pit of absolution, the absolute precision of a dream, a sleep-waking, a Hell-not-a-hell, though no false hell, for all's a false hell but exclusion from the Earth, and Heaven then is either ripening in the soil or it is Hell as certain as a Heaven. World and underworld then, and if the world is round then through logic one may find that under the sphere is the center, the zero, the nothing and the nothing-there, nether-world, never world, darksome hole, yes, love-hole, center of the flapping cry.

Words for women, death for men.

And the sparrow. Out of her came compathy. Not empathy, impossible to feel for, to feel into, to feel of. Who in Hell are you? Where are you? What? Huh? Dashed upon the rocks is all other consciousness. Only my consciousness of an other remains (and remember this is the birth of fear, the other, and so the world—*Genesis*, the *Upanishads*). There you are, looking like my sadness, and so I am sad alongside you, with you, on the shore, staring at sky or sea, ceaseless waves out there, sad at the same time, for what we cannot share. Only the words to share, and time, maybe.

Then on to irony. The laughing between. Let it slide off. Let truth to Hell and only the beauty of the lie remain in this upper world, this cavity of forgiveness (a lie) and love (a lie we make into birds): Sparrow! Irony makes the stilled wings flutter with my heartbeat! Compathy in positive capability. To make the world live as I am sad. Sadness my greatest irony—boy of joy, golden in all rapture. Sieve of nothing, conceiving the world. Irony does not work, but will birth us. I birth myself nightly in the bath of dream. I birth my sex, my weight, endlessly sinking through the weightless world, no stopping, though irony gives the many contraptions their voices and their space to wing. I fly though I sink. You are a heart I hold, and so destroy.

For there it is, the first law, gravity, pulling down. Science is Dionysian in its end, to ruins and into oblivion. Science will not accept a perfect symmetry, an eternity, as calculation denotes completion, but perfect balance is eternally incomplete, the colored scarves never ending from the dragon's mouth. That's the idea of joy, that it goes on forever, and it does. We get over sorrow so quickly in the petunias. And sex is the ache that refuses to end, the love of the ache, the breakless beak of the ache. The bird pecking my ear in Hell-that-is-Heaven, the bird of Lazarus inflicting self unto self: I know it is, and so I am content in the otherness, finally (this can only happen in death, I think). The gravity-Hell. The Hell of space-time. The Hell of Now. Now Here. Nowhere. Ear.

And through the ear, sorrow. The call of the other Out There. Outer, the condensation of her. She becomes a philosophy, and all philosophy leads to self, Self without her, and Self without all is incomplete, turning to the self-insignificant, the less-lessness of being one's self, neither outer nor inner, haunted by all, speechless in the cavity of receding. In ear. The words going out are not received, we think, I think. No you, for who is me? The cycles of god, these are, doubting presence. Death ends this. That is not certain. Not just things falling apart. Entropy of even the thought of entropy. All thought spews into hope and then hopelessly into a hope that matter can hold.

There God falls and out of the dust comes Urizen, holding his scepter, having thwarted beauty into the nether-abyss. We can only hold that the nether-abyss loves all beauty and so makes death a womb. Dear God, We made Us and you destroyed what was left. Our reason kills, like the morning light. There's a girl in a flowered dress dancing in the highland fields who is dead. There's a last blink of light in the eye and then slow thunder. We make Hell to cast us out of We. We make Heaven to hate Here. We sex to die. We die to not have been. To not matter. Matter is all disease when we breathe. The world goes dark when we blink. When we wake it is only a survival of night. What is out there, on the landscape of the barren plain? Just the cracking of electric reigns.

Then down, phoenix, a fancy, a deceit, a lie, a spark in the desert entirely possible, like the first life. We fashion us again. No fear of disaster. Leave out all that is true and beautiful. What is new and possible. What is makeable. What is fun and interesting. What keeps us awake. What makes us not hate We. O, there it is, and here I am failing, for I am uncertain where and, like Cocteau, cannot ask the way. And I have not found my Master, nor Guide, nor Slave, to lead me into that dark forge from where I know They come to save us. Look at the Golden Ones, flowering molten from the Dark unventured. Where shall we?

Wall Chart

Leaves and wind
In their vague nightly synthesis
Unable to sustain a memory
Or conflate a distinct moment

Here in the room with the machines turned off
And the windows cracked
The tearing of the stars lingers
Too long to influence
The floor unscrubbed
No sentence can turn the husband back to bed

In another house
The children have dreamed of murders
I walk past each front door and understand
The disaster simplified by economics

First cut off one finger
Then the entirety of poetry must go

Ruled by the Absence of Knowing

Perhaps a strangled doll should trouble
A dad who walks foot to foot who
Bounces check to check and rent
Disengaged thought from platitude

A dad who spends his time eating
What the kid doesn't eat and watching
What the kid watches and walking
As far as he can convince
The kid is far enough for now

A dad doesn't use metaphors
To fix the broken doll or to explain
That when the bike path gets steep

A dad can only sometimes carry
A kid a bike and a busted doll

Clearings

I

Hence a declension in the bucket's clime
Sings forth the atmosphere

Not comfortable in clearings
The figures run to small shadows

Birds do not despair
Drone strikes for
They have no minds
Our minds imply

II

I have seen language
In which a fork takes
Its space above us

What we call anything
Does not matter

A rotting song becomes this us

The computer crashing
Elates the room with unexpected light

III

Punctual always the raccoons
Scratch and eat behind the walls

Last night I heard something
Kill something while I fixated
On drone strikes in my Twitter feed

To do away with the sickness words carry
The penitent must penetrate doom as a joke
Penetrates a widow

Naked in their shapes
Every thought belongs to the floor in this room

The birds at four AM
Attach my reckoning to the cold
Though it is June
And I remember other Junes
The way sobs do

Member Brain

I

Detour left will not lead
That's what I do daily rather than eat
Why question
When you can linger at the train station like a gas chamber
I have heard poets say they do not dream
Rather than rhetoric I use these words
Many of you
And there are only a dozen in the room
Do not
You are not poets
I only know the better option was to become a flower
I did that poorly but poverty did justice for me
I don't have to admit I know nothing
But I will and won't fake it with imagery

II

The road map that's what some come in here for
I can't even find my way to the road
I'm sleeping on
I remember yesterday she told me about good poetry
By explaining how bad it was
Listen to that fear
And do not fear
And do not snicker
In that poem you will find the door at the end of your life
It does not help to stare
And blink
It will not go away once you see it
And it will not close once you open it
This is the book you have been reading
Set down

III

What I hear makes its own creations
It does not get any less comfortable living in the mind
When the mind can make what I hear
Make desperate sounds
Listen to the mind's ease
I tell my mind
Even when I have to tell it with my hand
I make the mind obey this vehement body
Precipice of the imagined
Ground I walk on
Feet unable to agree with the earth
This is not walking
Walking into a morning of its own shape

Relent

The old drunk in the park said
What I had felt about nearness

Negating intimacy not in those words
But as a donkey speaking

Ridiculous therefore incorrect
Multiple-choice en route to the bar

Where they don't allow carry-ins
And without an opener I smashed the neck on a bench

And chugged half of it half-carefully
My full identity disclosed to the failing sun

Though to myself I was just an asshole under a streetlamp
Who saw the leering drunk but would not share

Our common disease
A pair of fruits rotting in distant baskets

Because I would have told the asshole
Who made a shitnest of his angel-life

This lack of proximity you taught me
Makes us brothers and foulmouthed lovers

Deflected Light

Sufficient looking out at the drawbridge
Too bored to read

Too tired to walk up to the rooftop
Only to stare off into Queens

Which might as well have been on fire
For all the reality I cared for

No money then whether working or not
I let my wife go to work

And destroyed myself morning into afternoon
Recovery in washing a few dishes

And sneaking off to happy hour where I
Slit my wrists from the insides

I have a scar from a box cutter
An accident in a sober afterlife

Not unhappy not blindly fucking my eyes against the wall
Understand if you want the drawbridge relieved

That ridiculous yawn
Cars stalled there

The horrible air above Newtown Creek
If you want to believe something else

Walk away from this poem
Written with petroleum and burnt offerings

VERY SMALL BOOK

I

A VERY SMALL BOOK
Has windows in its pages

In my drawer
Cheap plastic
Parallelism
Don't pray to

Sirloin
Has no fingers

II

I remember my creative days
Necessary components of the disaster
That never came not even when the war
Never came not even the winter
Everyone stopped making love
Near the end of my creativity

In the midst of beautiful snow
I stopped writing letters when my typewriter broke
We moved away and the snow never fell
Except of course on the cold days
But the snow never stayed
The earth has become a fire

III

I have a scab from an insect bite on my tonsure
Every act eventually becomes self-referential

Gorgeous 3 PM sunlight
Hits the neighbor's aluminum roof

When I look back from my cat
Just ordinary sun in the leaves
And the neighbor's house looks
Sleepy as in dead

We call anything
Anything we want
All the leaves look taken

IV

I ate a small flower I don't know the name of
Not difficult to get comfortable in this world
As long as this is not the world

Stories don't have anything to do
If I stand a few feet back from the phone booth
On the projector screen

Not Parable

One says to her: do the math.

The other places her fork on the table and a billion registers clink out a warning shot, which the one who said do the math experiences as a flick to his temple, only now the one who placed her fork on the table knows it's a bullet, which doesn't surprise her given the escalating local conflict (she knows the assailant) but the cracking and the spatter still in the air shock her, though that hot rain will settle on her face, on her white blouse, on her eggs, and in her water glass.

Blood in water will squid dance and then spread itself sleepily into a haze too dissipated to resemble wine, though we long for that image.

The situation has been taken from our instincts. The language on this page, especially, disturbs our chance at believing in the reality of this event in a place above actual ground, in a room with boards that need scrubbing.

The language of this poem is not local to the event. None have her mind. Some will try where I have failed, to feel her body as she actually felt it, as the first shock ended, as her body settled into its weight, pulled down against the air that tried to detain her and hang her, slightly, in her unnatural position.

Everything Is about to Be Better than It Has Ever Been

The head's never-ending nonsense will end
With the body's finite pleasure

I suppose aphorism
Retains an erotomanic nostalgia
Akin to vocabulary
Thefted from essays by degraded thinkers

Masturbation needs no imagery

Emma Goldman walked a long dock once
Her thoughts did not cause the universe to spin

We can abide in resistance
Or indulge in such conventional possibilities
That in brief moments cosmos-tize us with zealots

Sometimes I have danced with zealots of unzealotry
I have gouged out the eyes of Moloch as he ate my face
My dreams have never taken me as far
As the writings of Marxists
At the shrunken lip above
Where dream-blackened subatomic mathematics
Writhes in serpentry
Marx himself relieves my masturbatory itch

I belong in a zoo really
But no one has written adroitly enough
To accomplish the radical freedom
Of the emerging poet in the failing imperialist state
As community-funded oddity in the public slammer
Flinging poo
Masturbating
Howling Stravinsky

Instead we have coffee shops
Funny hats in winter

I have always hated Townes van Zandt
And continue to emerge in my funny hatreds

I will not talk to anyone in this place
The blister of my silence will not immolate

As people lose their uses I begin to see the people
Their faces cannot be described by thought or sleep
No face will make one thousand trees explode
Every body is an instance of sex that will achieve release

Declaration in the Hours away from My Daughter

Now eating hurts and only God
Not existing brings the numbed possible

What angels
Says the street swept with brushes
Say the tax dollars
Lost on the street when the angels
Went drunk and suddenly dark
In the drowned mind

When a speaker puts the mind down finally
As the philosophers put down God
I can dream the mind
As capital walks
After Marx disfigured money
With flames and pitchforks

If only money would die
We could find a numb beginning
In a blanket of material
And our children could march
Beyond us into a world that spends only light

My daughter brays on a playground
In another part of town

I hold her toy frog as I write this
And own nothing

What holds us from holding our children
Is money and the law and the police
Who defend property
And who may someday
Defend me from my child
As if food or land or children
Could be property

Only the mind is property
Of no dead God
Of my child who is not crying out
Who is happy in her silence
Fighting her nap
And remembers I'll come before supper

Winter Separation Drinking Song

Dried out the mind
Talking with friends about the incomes of strange babies
With broken esophagi

When an ex finds a hammer
She might not say
She thinks a ghost smashed the mirror
The instant before she sees
The mirror in tact

When my ex speaks words an adolescent
Could blow off the page by reciting Celan
Or singing a miner's song
I prefer to have my daughter draw a picture on the empty side
And I tack it to the wall of the cave where I work

The world is made of cork
And sunlight adapts to wrong imagining
Because no imagining is wrong

Only the words are wrong
Even if the friends are right

I try to show it by saying it wrong
Then all the thoughts that have lifted my balloon head
Rain coal dust daughter sings
She loves the songs boozy white men stole

I don't begrudge her love of sounds
Of imperialism fashioned into
An art with implications below her thoughts
Which need no words

A child's thoughts are the world
They are literally the walls of light allowing her to see
And her words are the only words
That occur as I want my thoughts to find them
Barking in the cold laughter of each tiny sun she speaks

I Wrote This Song When I Lived in a Dumpster

I found your poem when I lived
In the trashcan I made my heart

My voice found its usefulness
When I scraped out the bullshit

With a fountain pen and burned
Off the resin with a Bic lighter

Your mother stopped answering my texts
But the light is on in your room

And all of this happens in my head
I never stalked you once I lost

The desire to hack into your email
When I realized I'd die if I spent

One more night drinking fire, huffing
Dark matter and gasoline

Are You Mad at Me?

I am alone in a room deciding what to say to the room

There is crazy that recognizes itself and crazy without a clue

I would never have understood the noise without the dancing

The best part of smoking crack was divorce

This poem is composed of tweets I should not have deleted

Paid, fucked, and fed

I got sober and forgot how to spell

This poem is an absence in place of the Nina Simone song
I could not disambiguate

We all wear one black dress into our whoredom

Made my bed two mornings in a row, an all-time record

I haven't had a drink in seventy days

I don't think of you doing anything I want to know about

I can mostly wake up before daybreak and watch the daybreak

I don't want to hurt you with this immense happiness that
fucks me all day

Like the air fucked Whitman's ears

I want to write this poem however and disintegrate you

I will do this instead of doing the things you have nevertheless
said I have done

My aesthetic is broken because your shitty living forced me to
become whole

To get away from you I had to ride a horse made of someone
else's bullshit

I had to ask God for things from the place where there is no God

It was painful the way the cosmos burned me with hand jobs

The problem with therapy is it only reconfigures us into society

That place full of God and assholes with opinions about God

I prefer the place I rode to on someone else's bullshit where I
burned my scrotum

I say petty things to you out of consideration

Because you adore your petticoat

Which is just a word and all you have for a brain is words

Scarecrow to your own thoughts

I am sorry I never hung up on you

I am sorry there wasn't a star who fucked you

I am sorry you are lonely now with your birthday cake and your friends' attires

In your tired bone clothes that remind you

You were beautiful before you learned worship

Because you adore your mother more than your motherhood

Whatever I might be worried about can wait for the door to close

Because I have admitted these lines that are personal wretches

Cast as misogyny into my poetry

Which doesn't mean shit unless I admit every piece of shit

If you let me in your house often enough, I'll eat all the cookies

I just want to cook, fuck, and talk about feelings

How old folks still love their long-dead parents

Now I'm the sober single dad who lives behind a head shop in a tiny apartment

Full of books

My eyes out the window in a pink mess

Sky so blue, head so still

I Don't Get Home Much Anymore

Cancer stink on interstates through
Missouri and Illinois

No dreams induce sleep

Home
The word

Represents
Proximity to grass and trees
A mind away from smoke

The home I lived in
All the streets coordinate
Paralysis in a shot of strychnine

Now I prefer stoned mountain roads
I live in a box in the mountains, yes
But my parents don't cry in
Their words there

I broke their mouths against my door
I locked myself inside with my daughter and her laughter
The shotgun I hold to my head

My light-crazed head
Grins in the trees
Shining through the window

I've been told to stop talking about light
To think money language
To think military-industrial complex squid children shudders
To drop drones everywhere

But light, friends, enters through the windows
Without breaking anything
Light makes the trees and light makes
My daughter laugh

Not a weapon
My daughter

When the world is made of light

Mind glows its own solution
Mind not like moon, not reflecting

But origin, a child
Laughing when her daddy laughs

One bird laughing after another

I don't go home
What fire alights has burned out
What has resolved in its ash
Hardly holds anything

A house will not stand after emptying

Places away from the disasters
Let me breathe out

I open the door and let my daughter
Run down sidewalks full of commerce

The Story of God

I texted my ex and after a few days she responded with a nothing
That brought me back to nothing

I realize I am in love with poetry

This afternoon a blue jay flew up from the road
And away from the car
Then back at the car and nearly into the window

I said so to my daughter
In her car seat and she laughed and said Daddy that's a trick
And I tried to explain there are things we don't
See because of where we are sitting
I said sometimes birds fly into cars

And because I am in love with poetry and not
My own divorce I don't want what I said
To my daughter to mean anything

But unlike my ex my daughter responds
Laughing and she doesn't believe me when I say
Birds can fly into cars
And her laughing and my inability
To explain one small possible reality
Sort of let the car float for a moment
Above the daylight into a thicker liquid light

The metaphor can't relate to me if the initial image is just a trick
As my daughter says

We bought squirt guns and she ran
Around the park shooting trees
She shot up the trees and ran all over the grass
And climbed down to the creek and took off
Her shoes and walked in the water
And threw the biggest rocks she could lift from the creek
Back into the creek bed

I watched her as I held my phone
And wanted to tell her that she is a trick
That blue jays are not real
And the creek is not full of water
That she cannot throw a rock into the same creek once

When she has grown tired of the wind beating her car
As she drives on the interstate away from a disaster
I can't imagine now, I imagine
She will see that the past is empty of us
And the world unfolds until it isn't a world
Just lint from someone else's hamper

But how do we throw that away
When it's the world

Afterlife with a Gentle Afterward

All my time has been a reed
I dreamed in a blackout

It turns out every sun
Has been a different sun
Every sky
Has lied about continuity

Every blink
Has blanked
The light behind

I figured
Myself against the horizon

One could see my shape only

Every face exists for at least one illusion

Somehow the light turns around
The face becomes a sun
The eyes become a sky

I am saying so directly to you
In your light which is blinking
And burning what will not burn out

Kaveh's Window

The song is tired, friend
In the aftermath of polyphonic fuck ups
On a Thursday night with the wind out and the stars down
Dead pigeons near a vodka bottle in the berm

When you come back, let's watch a movie
Hungarians dancing after closing time
The darkest choose mad disaster over terminal sorrow

I have come to believe the only good people are poor
In my stubborn religion I deny all contrary evidence

I tried believing nothing and it got me nothing
But I woke up after ten minutes' sleep
In the apartment you gave me for two weeks

Only a friend would not ask me to describe
The trees out your window in winter light
Orange and blue and white light in the ice

Because you have been there, Kaveh
Because you have slept in that bed and lived to tell about it

I saw the squirrel this morning
On the roof below your window
And for a moment I wanted to say something

To anyone, and I suppose that
Is where religion begins
The house we must enter
When we close the final door

There is no world until all our friends arrive there

V

Defense

Saved from salvation by fettered sex
I look at my hands
Because she always says to look at my hands

Nothing happens because there is no God
And when she tells me to pray
I pray to the darkest spot of oblivion

I woke once on my bedroom floor
The sliding door open
A bird flew in
I thought There's a bird on the dresser

I maintained the thing over there
Was proof of someone else's joy
I had heard of in a bar
And kin to something I had snorted
In a bathroom I never fully made it out of
Part of my brain splattered on a tray

She tells me now we don't really go back
We look at our hands and I say
It doesn't work but after a few days
I look at my ripped up shins and knees

My leg went through a roof once
I wrapped it up in the shirt I had worn all day
And drank a big can of beer on the drive home
My wife was pregnant on the couch
I said of the beer This is my medicine
I might as well have been slitting our throats
But the baby came
And someone else paid for the delivery

No one came to take the baby away
My hands filled with love and I thought
I could make my body a balloon
And fill it with nothing and make nothing look like love
But it was easier to fill it with whiskey and cocaine

Now I wonder if I ever made my wife smile
Awake all night making bullshit on my computer
Pretending I was going to stay sober
Drinking kerosene straight from my brain
Sucking resin from my smoked out interior

She tells me I am leaving that body behind
I have new hands but when I look at my legs
I see I have them I can walk
I am not falling through the roof now

I hold out my hands and see the world become like my hands

I wake up mid-February a few weeks sober
And watch dark morning crack into pinks and yellows
And I look at the light like I hold out my hands
And in this cult of myself I decree myself obliterated

Which of course only half happens
My audacity clings to my words
Like I have been eating from a cob

Or it is that I can only say so in a huff
Eating through cobwebs to get to the spider who is gone

So I shower because this is the hour my lover comes over
And my lover loves my body clean
My whiskers a day old my candles lit
And nothing to do but talk and eat cantaloupe
And kiss and touch and fuck in the disorganized light
The candles break on our walls and on our faces

Everywhere we have lived gazing into one light-changing face
What I thought that bird was

So I will wash my body again with hot water and soap
And wait for my lover now even after she has broken it off

Because I am getting older every time I let
My eyesight fall apart every time I wait
For someone else to come other than
Myself standing outside myself

Where my hands were when she told me to look
Or my lover's body pressing up
As I pressed down and we met in broken
Blessing as if flowers could crush into each other
By volition and press their dye into light

I pray into the first lit spot of day
Alone in my bed
Pressing into the cushion beneath me
Pressing into the air above and around me
Pressing into what I am thinking and breathing
And pressing into what I am not yet
Until an absence of feeling lifts
And drops and finally unhooks me

Until I am not even that corpse
In the river not even my atoms
Broken up into parts of the river
And parts of the earth and parts
Of the sky until I am departed
Not by fire but by choice to be
Washed away from the world
Against my will and to wipe

The world away as I go into
What once I saw as awful sadness
And which now I do not see but am

Acknowledgments

My gratitude to Joe Morra and the Boomerang Fund for Artists, who provided me with a grant that helped me complete this book. My gratitude also to an anonymous group of poets who came up with a sum of money that got my daughter and me through the dark times in which much of this book was written. Infinite gratitude to Joshua Ware, whose hyper-illuminated text, *iSun*, of my first book, *Ordinary Sun*, made me believe in my own poetry at a time when I needed it to help me survive.

Thank you to C. Violet Eaton and Sara Nicholson for seeing these poems and this book through many edits and for seeing me through the darkness, and to Suedee Hall Elkins, Nicole Fares, and Kaveh Bassiri, for whom friendship is not an adequate word.

Thanks also to the following people for helping me with matters of poetry or of my person: Andrea Baker, Stephanie Balzer, Lily Brown, Cody-Rose Clevidence, Geffrey Davis, Tim Earley, Stacy England, Emily Kendal Frey, Jane Gregory, Susana Gardner, Whit Griffin, Rauan Klassnik, Justin Marks, Katie Nichol, Hung Pham, Brandon Shimoda, Samantha Sigmon, Sandra Simonds, Mark Spitzer, Deborah Woodard, Timmy Ussery, and Tim Van Dyke.

Thanks again to Carrie Olivia Adams, Nikkita Cohoon, Janaka Stucky, and all the Black Ocean folks.

All love to my family; to my brothers in poetry, Adam Clay and Shannon Jonas; to my partner in existence, Molly O'Meara; and always to my daughter, Adele Cecilia Henriksen, brilliant and kind-hearted to the core.

"Not Parable" is for Nicole Fares.

"Defense" is for Emily Kendal Frey.

The phrase "I wrote this song when I lived in a dumpster" comes from Tom Waits.

Agriculture Reader: "Are You Mad at Me?" "I Wrote This Song When I Lived in a Dumpster," "Ruled by an Absence of Knowing," and "Winter Separation Drinking Song"

Ampersand Review: "Declaration in the Hours Away from My Daughter"

Apartment: "Requiem for Now" and "Stereo Gone"

Bright Pink Mosquito: "Strange Flowers"

Brooklyn Rail: "Everything Is about to Be Better than It Ever Has Been," "Kaveh's Window," "Not Parable," and "Sweetness and Milk"

The Cultural Society: "Therapy Poem"

The Equalizer: "VERY SMALL BOOK"

Fence: "Member Brain"

HTML Giant: "I Don't Get Home Much Anymore"

Mandorla: "Relent" and "Deflected Light"

Map Literary: "The Story of God"

N/A: "I Throw Rocks"

No Infinite: "Afterlife with a Gentle Afterward"

The Pinch: "Defense"

Pretty Lit: "Clearings"

The Rumpus: "Sober Lullaby"

So & So Magazine: "Baby"

Timber Journal: "Wall Chart"

Yalobusha Review: "People Say This is Not Music"

"My W/hole Aesthetic" appeared as a self-published
    pamphlet from Cannibal Books during The Frank
    Stanford Literary Festival in Fayetteville, Arkansas in
    October of 2008.